Cooking Korean Dishes at Home

Simple but Flavorful Korean Recipes You'd Love

BY: SOPHIA FREEMAN

Table of Contents

Introduction

Craving for Korean dishes but don't want to leave the house?

Here's the good news: you can now make your own delicious and healthy Korean dishes in the comfort of your own home, with the help of this handy cookbook.

Here are just a few of the many recipes that you'll find in this book:

Kimchi

Kimchi is dubbed as "quintessential" to almost every Korean meal that you'll have. Yes, there are many versions of Kimchi, but in this book, you'll find the most popular one made with Napa cabbage.

Samgyeopsal

Samgyeopsal is grilled pork belly that's bursting with so many flavors you can't get enough of.

Bulgogi

This one is another famous delicacy in Korea, in which you will barbecue strips of chicken, beef or pork.

Stews and Soups

There are so many choices when it comes to Korean stews and soups. But for sure, you'll love all those that are provided in this book. Most of these are made with natural broths, veggies, herbs and spices.

You don't have to travel all the way to South Korea to get a taste of their rich and interesting cuisine. You simply have to visit an Asian food store to get the ingredients that you need and start preparing one of the dishes from this book at your very own kitchen.

Get started right away!

Korean Barbecue Steak

Soak your beef flank steak in a tasty marinade for 6 hours. After that, cook the steak on the grill, and serve with bok choy. Fancy dinner doesn't get any simpler than this.

Serving Size: 6

Preparation & Cooking Time: 6 hours and 40 minutes

Ingredients:

- 1 tablespoon ginger, grated
- 3 cloves garlic, crushed and minced
- 2 tablespoons brown sugar
- ¼ cup low-sodium soy sauce
- 1 tablespoon sesame oil, toasted
- 1 lb. flank steak, fat trimmed and scored
- 3 cups bok choy, chopped and steamed
- 2 tablespoons green onion, chopped
- 1 tablespoon white sesame seeds, toasted

Instructions:

Place the ginger, garlic, brown sugar, soy sauce and sesame oil in a large bowl.

Add the steak and coat evenly with the sauce.

Cover and marinate in the refrigerator for 6 hours.

Preheat your grill.

Grill the steak for 10 minutes.

Flip and grill for another 10 minutes.

Serve with the bok choy and garnish with the green onion and sesame seeds.

Nutrients per Serving:

- Calories 194
- Fat 7.7 g
- Saturated fat 2.6 g
- Carbohydrates 4.2 g
- Fiber 0.6 g
- Protein 25.5 g
- Cholesterol 68 mg
- Sugars 3 g
- Sodium 276 mg
- Potassium 496 mg

Korean Beef in Cabbage Cups

This isn't just an eye candy. It's also bursting with so many incredible flavors. Making the beef ultra tasty is the combination of brown sugar, chili sauce, ginger, rice vinegar and sesame seeds.

Serving Size: 8

Preparation Cooking Time: 8 hours and 20 minutes

Ingredients:

- 2 lb. chuck roast (boneless), cubed
- ¼ cup all-purpose flour
- 1 ½ tablespoons sesame oil
- Cooking spray
- 8 garlic cloves, peeled and crushed
- 1 tablespoon ginger, minced
- ½ cup rice vinegar
- 3 tablespoons reduced-sodium soy sauce
- 3 tablespoons brown sugar
- ¼ cup sesame seeds
- Salt to taste
- 2 tablespoons hot sauce
- 16 cabbage leaves
- Scallions, chopped

Instructions:

Coat the beef cubes with the flour.

Add the sesame oil to a pan over medium heat.

Cook the beef cubes for 6 to 8 minutes.

Spray your slow cooker with oil.

Transfer these to your pot.

Cook the garlic in the pan for 1 minute.

Transfer the garlic to the slow cooker.

In a bowl, mix the ginger, vinegar, soy sauce, brown sugar, sesame seeds, salt and hot sauce.

Pour the mixture into the slow cooker.

Cover the pot.

Cook on low for 8 hours.

Pour the cooking liquid through a strainer.

Discard the solids.

Add the beef on top of the cabbage leaves.

Garnish each with the scallions.

Drizzle the cooking liquid on top and serve.

Nutrients per Serving:

- Calories 255
- Fat 10 g
- Saturated fat 2 g
- Carbohydrates 13 g
- Fiber 2 g
- Protein 28 g
- Cholesterol 102 mg
- Sugars 6 g
- Sodium 575 mg
- Potassium 780 mg

Korean Beef with Kimchi Stew

The combination of brown sugar and Kimchi lend a unique taste to this Korean stew. It's filling, comforting and delicious. Plus, it's also a cinch to make. Despite the long cooking hours, it actually only takes a few minutes of active preparation.

Serving Size: 8

Preparation Cooking Time: 7 hours and 40 minutes

Ingredients:

- 1 tablespoon vegetable oil
- 2 lb. beef chuck roast (boneless), fat trimmed
- 3 tablespoons reduced-sodium soy sauce
- ¼ cup dry white wine
- 3 tablespoons brown sugar
- 4 cups chicken broth
- 6 cloves garlic, crushed and minced
- 1 jalapeño chili, chopped
- 1 yellow onion, sliced into quarters
- 14 oz. Napa cabbage, chopped
- Salt and pepper to taste
- ¾ cup Kimchi
- 2 scallions, sliced thinly

Instructions:

Pour the oil into a pan over medium heat.

Cook the beef for 10 minutes.

Place the beef in the slow cooker.

Pour the soy sauce and wine into the pan.

Stir in the brown sugar and bring to a boil.

Transfer the mixture to the slow cooker.

Add the broth, garlic, chili and onion to the pot.

Cover the pot and cook on low for 7 hours.

Take the beef out of the pot and shred.

Put the beef back to the pot along with the cabbage.

Season with salt and pepper.

Seal the pot and cook on low for 10 minutes.

Pour into serving bowls and top with the Kimchi and scallions.

Nutrients per Serving:

- Calories 225
- Fat 7 g
- Saturated fat 2 g
- Carbohydrates 11 g
- Fiber 1 g
- Protein 28 g
- Cholesterol 101 mg
- Sugars 7 g
- Sodium 634 mg
- Potassium 556 mg

Korean Rice Bowls

There are many variations when it comes to making the Korean rice bowl. In this one, we put together beef, Kimchi and egg, and serve all these on top of cauliflower rice.

Serving Size: 4

Preparation Cooking Time: 30 minutes

Ingredients:

- 4 tablespoons sesame oil, divided
- 1 tablespoon ginger, minced
- 2 stalks scallions, sliced
- 6 cups cauliflower rice
- Salt to taste
- 1 lb. sirloin steak, sliced thinly
- 2 tablespoons sesame seeds, toasted
- ¼ cup gochujang
- ½ cup Kimchi
- 1 cup carrots, shredded
- 2 hard-boiled eggs, peeled and sliced in half

Instructions:

Pour half of the oil into a pan over medium heat.

Cook the ginger, scallions, cauliflower and salt for 5 minutes, stirring frequently.

Transfer the rice to a bowl.

Cover with foil.

Pour the remaining oil to another pan.

Cook the steak for 4 minutes.

Remove from the stove.

Stir in the sesame seeds and gochujang.

Transfer the cauliflower rice in serving bowls.

Top with the steak, egg slices, Kimchi, carrots, and eggs.

Nutrients per Serving:

- Calories 414
- Fat 22.9 g
- Saturated fat 4.7 g
- Carbohydrates 20 g
- Fiber 5.5 g
- Protein 30.4 g
- Cholesterol 152 mg
- Sugars 9 g
- Sodium 720 mg
- Potassium 388 mg

Korean Lettuce Wraps

Healthy, delicious and full of flavor—there's nothing more you can ask from this amazing recipe that only takes 20 minutes to prepare.

Serving Size: 4

Preparation Cooking Time: 20 minutes

Ingredients:

- 12 oz. lean ground beef
- 2 teaspoons sesame oil, toasted
- 3 tablespoons low-sodium soy sauce
- 1 tablespoon chili garlic sauce
- 12 oz. broccoli slaw mix, shredded
- 8 large lettuce leaves
- ½ cup red bell pepper, chopped

Instructions:

Cook the ground beef in a pan over medium heat until brown.

Add the sesame oil, soy sauce and chili garlic to the pan.

Add the broccoli slaw.

Cook for 3 minutes.

Add the mixture on top of the lettuce leaves.

Sprinkle the bell pepper on top.

Roll up the lettuce leaves and secure using toothpicks.

Nutrients per Serving:

- Calories 185
- Fat 6.6 g
- Saturated fat 2.2 g
- Carbohydrates 8.9 g
- Fiber 2.6 g
- Protein 21.3 g
- Cholesterol 53 mg
- Sugars 5 g
- Sodium 567 mg
- Potassium 356 mg

Kimchi

It's always a good idea to make Kimchi. You can serve this with most main courses. You can also add this to your stews or sandwiches.

Serving Size: 32

Preparation Cooking Time: 4 days

Ingredients:

- 2 lb. Napa cabbage, sliced into 1-inch pieces
- ¼ cup salt
- Water
- 4 scallions, chopped
- 2 cups daikon radish, sliced into strips
- 1 teaspoon sugar
- ¼ cup ginger, sliced into strips
- 2 cloves garlic, sliced into quarters
- 2 tablespoons fish sauce
- 3 tablespoons red pepper flakes

Instructions:

Toss the cabbage in salt in a bowl.

Add a little water just enough to submerge the cabbage.

Cover and let sit for 24 hours.

Remove the cabbage from the water. Reserve the brine.

Squeeze the cabbage dry.

Place on a bowl and stir in the scallions and daikon.

In a food processor, add the sugar, ginger, garlic, fish sauce and red pepper.

Pulse until smooth.

Add to the cabbage.

Massage until well mixed.

Transfer to a glass jar with lid.

Pour in the brine.

Seal and let sit for 3 days.

Store in the refrigerator.

Nutrients per Serving:

- Calories 9
- Fat 0.1 g
- Saturated fat 0 g
- Carbohydrates 1.6 g
- Fiber 0.7 g
- Protein 0.6 g
- Cholesterol 20 mg
- Sugars 1 g
- Sodium 104 mg
- Potassium 97 mg

Korean Barbecue Tofu

Here's one Korean recipe vegetarians will find hard to resist—grilled tofu glazed with Korean barbecue sauce and served with chopped cabbage and scallions.

Serving Size: 4

Preparation Cooking Time: 9 hours

Ingredients:

Tofu and Sauce

- 15 oz. tofu, sliced
- 3 tablespoons peanut oil, divided
- ½ cup onion, chopped
- 2 tablespoons ginger, minced
- 2 tablespoons garlic, minced
- ¾ cup scallions, chopped
- 2 tablespoons gochujang
- 2 tablespoons water
- ¼ cup low-sodium soy sauce
- 2 tablespoons rice vinegar
- 2 tablespoons paprika
- 2 teaspoons molasses
- 1 tablespoon sesame oil, toasted
- 2 teaspoons white miso
- 1 tablespoon honey

Cabbage

- 2 tablespoons sesame oil, toasted
- 3 tablespoons low-sodium soy sauce
- 2 tablespoons peanut oil
- 1 ½ cups scallions, chopped
- 12 cups Napa cabbage, chopped
- 2 tablespoons sesame seeds

Instructions:

Arrange the tofu on a clean surface.

Place a kitchen towel on top of slices of tofu.

Add a baking pan on top.

Place a heavy object on top of the baking pan to squeeze the moisture out of the tofu.

Let stand for 4 hours.

After 4 hours, pour 1 tablespoon peanut oil to a pan over medium heat.

Cook the onion for 5 minutes.

Add the ginger and garlic. Cook for 1 minute.

Remove from the stove.

Transfer to a bowl.

Stir in the remaining sauce ingredients in a bowl.

Add 1 tablespoon sesame oil.

Mix well.

Brush the tofu slices with this mixture.

Marinate for 4 hours.

Preheat your grill.

Grill the tofu for 5 minutes per side.

Keep warm while preparing the cabbage.

In a bowl, mix the sesame oil and soy sauce.

Pour the peanut oil into a pan over high heat.

Cook the scallions for 3 minutes.

Stir in the cabbage and cook for 3 minutes.

Pour in the soy sauce mixture and sesame seeds.

Serve the grilled tofu with the stir-fried cabbage.

Nutrients per Serving:

- Calories 389
- Fat 31 g
- Saturated fat 5 g
- Carbohydrates 18.5 g
- Fiber 7.2 g
- Protein 16.3 g
- Cholesterol 56 mg
- Sugars 5 g
- Sodium 759 mg
- Potassium 871 mg

Fish with Tamari Chili Sauce

One of the easiest Korean fish recipes you'll find—this one is made by cooking the fish in tamari chili sauce. Serve with brown rice or steamed veggies.

Serving Size: 4

Preparation Cooking Time: 30 minutes

Ingredients:

- 3 tablespoons rice vinegar
- 3 tablespoons brown sugar
- 1 tablespoon water
- ¼ cup reduced-sodium tamari
- 3 tablespoons olive oil, divided
- 1 Korean chili pepper, chopped
- 2 cloves garlic, minced
- 1 tablespoon sesame oil, toasted
- 1 ¼ lb. cod, sliced into 4
- Pepper to taste
- Sesame seeds

Instructions:

In a bowl, mix the vinegar, sugar, water and tamari.

Pour 1 tablespoon olive oil into a pan over medium heat.

Cook the chili and garlic for 1 minute.

Pour in the vinegar mixture.

Simmer for 10 minutes or until reduced in half.

Remove from the stove.

Stir in the sesame oil.

Season the fish with pepper.

Add the remaining olive oil into the pan.

Cook the fish for 3 minutes.

1Top with the sauce and garnish with the sesame seeds.

Nutrients per Serving:

- Calories 268
- Fat 14.4 g
- Saturated fat 2.1 g
- Carbohydrates 12.1 g
- Fiber 0.2 g
- Protein 20.5 g
- Cholesterol 56 mg
- Sugars 10 g
- Sodium 770 mg
- Potassium 302 mg

Seaweed Soup

In the old days, this soup was used as pain relief for mothers who have just given birth. But you don't have to be a new mom to enjoy this comforting and delicious Korean soup.

Serving Size: 8

Preparation Cooking Time: 1 hour and 5 minutes

Ingredients:

- Cold water
- 2 cups miyuk (brown seaweed), sliced into small pieces
- 3 teaspoons sesame oil, toasted and divided
- 2 tablespoons low-sodium tamari
- 6 cloves garlic, shredded
- 8 oz. chicken thighs (boneless and skinless), sliced into strips
- 8 cups reduced-sodium chicken broth
- Sesame seeds

Instructions:

Fill a bowl with cold water.

Soak the miyuk in this bowl for 30 minutes.

Drain and rinse.

In a bowl, mix 2 teaspoons oil with the tamari and garlic.

Toss the chicken strips in this mixture.

Marinate for 15 minutes.

Pour the remaining oil in a pan over medium heat.

Cook the chicken for 1 minute.

Stir in the seaweed and cook for 3 minutes.

Pour in the broth.

Bring to a boil.

Skim the fat.

Reduce heat and simmer for 30 minutes.

Garnish with the sesame seeds.

Nutrients per Serving:

- Calories 110
- Fat 5.2 g
- Saturated fat 1.2 g
- Carbohydrates 5.3 g
- Fiber 1.5 g
- Protein 11.4 g
- Cholesterol 19 mg
- Sugars 1 g
- Sodium 497 mg
- Potassium 424 mg

Ssamjang

You'll find many uses for this tasty Korean sauce. You can spread this on lettuce leaves, drizzle on steamed veggies, or serve with grilled meat or chicken.

Serving Size: 16

Preparation Cooking Time: 5 minutes

Ingredients:

- 1 clove garlic, grated
- ¼ cup mirin
- ½ cup doenjang
- 2 teaspoons sesame oil, toasted
- 2 tablespoons sesame seeds, toasted
- 3 tablespoons gochujang

Instructions:

Combine all the ingredients in a bowl.

Store the sauce for up to 1 week in the refrigerator.

Nutrients per Serving:

- Calories 41
- Fat 1.5 g
- Saturated fat 0.2 g
- Carbohydrates 4.9 g
- Fiber 0.6 g
- Protein 1.3 g
- Cholesterol 10 mg
- Sugars 3 g
- Sodium 300 mg
- Potassium 5 mg

Korean Barbecue Short Ribs

You're going to fall madly in love with these savory short ribs that are infused with a little bit of sweet flavor.

Serving Size: 4

Preparation Cooking Time: 2 hours and 30 minutes

Ingredients:

Ribs

- 3 tablespoons low-sodium tamari
- 3 cloves garlic, grated
- 1 pear, grated
- 2 teaspoons fresh ginger, grated
- 1 tablespoon brown sugar
- Pepper to taste
- 2 tablespoons sesame oil, toasted
- 6 beef short ribs, fat trimmed

Serving

- 12 lettuce leaves
- Kimchi
- ¼ cup Ssamjang
- 3 cups brown rice, cooked

Instructions:

In a large bowl, mix the tamari, garlic, pear, ginger, sugar, pepper and sesame oil.

Cover the bowl.

Marinate the ribs in this mixture for 2 hours in the refrigerator.

Preheat your grill.

Grill the ribs for 5 minutes per side.

Let rest for 10 minutes before slicing.

Serve with the lettuce, Kimchi, ssamjang and brown rice.

Nutrients per Serving:

- Calories 514
- Fat 21.7 g
- Saturated fat 7.6 g
- Carbohydrates 44.8 g
- Fiber 4.7 g
- Protein 32.3 g
- Cholesterol 79 mg
- Sugars 6 g
- Sodium 621 mg
- Potassium 495 mg

Tofu Japchae Noodles

This popular Korean noodle dish is full of colors, textures and flavors. It's no wonder Japchae is much loved not only in Korea but also in other countries.

Serving Size: 6

Preparation Cooking Time: 1 hour and 15 minutes

Ingredients:

Tofu

- 14 oz. tofu
- Salt and pepper to taste
- 2 teaspoons vegetable oil

Eggs

- 1 teaspoon vegetable oil
- 2 eggs
- Salt to taste
- 1 tablespoon water

Sauce

- ¼ cup sesame oil, toasted
- ¼ cup sesame seeds, toasted and crushed
- 2 tablespoons low-sodium tamari
- ¼ cup brown sugar

Noodles

- Water
- 12 oz. glass noodles
- 2 tablespoons low-sodium tamari

Veggies

- 1 tablespoon vegetable oil
- 1 onion, sliced thinly
- 8 cups baby carrots, sliced
- 4 stalks red chard, sliced
- 6 broccolini, sliced in half
- 12 oyster mushrooms, sliced thinly
- 6 oz. snap peas, sliced
- ¼ cup green chives, chopped
- Black sesame seeds

Instructions:

Preheat your grill.

Press the tofu by placing a kitchen towel and baking pan on top.

Add weight to the baking pan and let sit for 15 minutes.

Slice the tofu into triangles.

Coat with the salt, pepper and oil.

Grill the tofu for 2 minutes per side.

Transfer to a bowl and set aside.

Prepare the eggs by pouring the oil into a pan over medium heat.

Beat the eggs in a bowl.

Stir in the salt and water.

Pour the eggs to the pan.

Let cook without stirring for 2 minutes.

Flip and cook for another 30 seconds.

Transfer the egg to a cutting board and slice into long strips. Set aside.

Mix the sauce ingredients in a bowl and set aside.

Prepare the noodles by boiling the glass noodles in a pot of water, following the directions in the package.

Toss in the tamari and set aside.

Prepare the veggies by pouring the vegetable oil to a pan over medium heat.

Cook the onion and carrots for 54 minutes.

Add the chard and broccolini.

Cook for 3 minutes.

Stir in the mushrooms and snap peas.

Cook for 3 minutes.

Stir in the chives and cook for 2 minutes.

Toss the noodles in the vegetables.

Transfer to serving bowls.

Top with the tofu and egg.

Garnish with the sesame seeds.

Nutrients per Serving:

- Calories 507
- Fat 21.8 g
- Saturated fat 3.1 g
- Carbohydrates 67.3 g
- Fiber 4 g
- Protein 13.3 g
- Cholesterol 62 mg
- Sugars 13 g
- Sodium 658 mg
- Potassium 486 mg

Pajeon

Pajeon is a popular savory pancake in Korea typically made with seafood and veggies. In this version, we'll be making one with shrimp and mushrooms.

Serving Size: 4

Preparation Cooking Time: 40 minutes

Ingredients:

- 2 tablespoons doenjang
- 6 tablespoons flour
- ¾ cup rice flour
- Salt and pepper to taste
- 1 ¼ cups cold water
- 5 oyster mushrooms, chopped
- 5 scallions, sliced thinly
- 4 oz. shrimps, peeling, deveining and slicing into small pieces
- 2 cloves garlic, grated
- 2 Korean chili, julienned
- 2 tablespoons olive oil, divided

Instructions:

Mix the doenjang, flour, rice flour, salt and pepper in a bowl.

Gradually add the water and mix until dissolved.

Add the rest of the ingredients except the olive oil.

Mix well.

Pour the oil into a pan over medium heat.

Pour ¼ cup of the batter.

Cook for 2 minutes per side or until golden.

Drain in a plate lined with paper towel.

Repeat the steps for the rest of the batter.

Nutrients per Serving:

- Calories 319
- Fat 8.9 g
- Saturated fat 1.3 g
- Carbohydrates 47.5 g
- Fiber 6.2 g
- Protein 15.4 g
- Cholesterol 40 mg
- Sugars 3 g
- Sodium 502 mg
- Potassium 950 mg

Kimchi, Noodles Shrimp

This is ideal for anyone who's craving for Korean dishes but don't have too much time to create elaborate meals. You can prepare this in advance and serve at any time during the week.

Serving Size: 3

Preparation Cooking Time: 15 minutes

Ingredients:

- 3 teaspoons low-sodium chicken bouillon paste
- 3 teaspoons gochujang
- 1 ½ cups mushrooms, sliced
- 1 ½ cups cabbage, chopped
- 9 oz. shrimp, cooked
- ¾ cup Kimchi, chopped
- 1 radish, sliced
- 1 ½ cups rice noodles, cooked
- 2 teaspoons cilantro, chopped
- 3 slices lime
- 3 cups boiling water

Instructions:

Divide the paste and gochujang into 3 glass jars with lid.

Layer the rest of the ingredients divided among the 3 jars.

Seal with the lid and refrigerate for up to 3 days.

Pour the boiling water into the jar when ready to serve.

Nutrients per Serving:

- Calories 239
- Fat 1.2 g
- Saturated fat 0.1 g
- Carbohydrates 31.8 g
- Fiber 3.3 g
- Protein 25.6 g
- Cholesterol 161 mg
- Sugars 5 g
- Sodium 926 mg
- Potassium 408 mg

Korean Chicken in Skewers

If you visit Korea, you'll find these chicken skewers as a popular street food delicacy. But you can also make your own at home using this simple-to-follow recipe.

Serving Size: 4

Preparation Cooking Time: 1 hour and 35 minutes

Ingredients:

- 2 tablespoons mirin
- 1 clove garlic, grated
- 1 tablespoon sesame oil, toasted
- 1 tablespoon low-sodium tamari
- 1 lb. chicken thigh fillet, sliced into 24 cubes
- Thick scallions, sliced into 24 pieces
- 12 shiitake mushrooms, sliced into half
- 2 tablespoons vegetable oil
- Salt to taste
- 6 tablespoons Ssamjang

Instructions:

Mix the garlic, sesame oil, tamari and mirin in a bowl.

Marinate the chicken for 1 hour, covered in the refrigerator.

Preheat your grill.

Toss the scallions and mushrooms in oil and salt.

Thread the chicken, mushrooms and scallions into the skewers.

Grill the skewers on each side for 3 minutes.

Serve with the ssamjang sauce.

Nutrients per Serving:

- Calories 329
- Fat 18.7 g
- Saturated fat 3.3 g
- Carbohydrates 14.1 g
- Fiber 3.1 g
- Protein 24.9 g
- Cholesterol 76 mg
- Sugars 7 g
- Sodium 686 mg
- Potassium 418 mg

Kimchi Fried Rice with Pork

In this simple and no-fuss Korean recipe, you will simply have to stir-fry the rice in Kimchi, pork cubes and veggies.

Serving Size: 4

Preparation Cooking Time: 35 minutes

Ingredients:

- 1 teaspoon peanut oil
- 2 eggs, beaten
- 2 tablespoons vegetable oil, divided
- 2 teaspoons garlic, minced
- 3 scallions, sliced thinly
- 2 teaspoons ginger, grated
- 1 lb. pork tenderloin, sliced into small pieces
- 1 cup carrots, diced
- 1 cup zucchini, diced
- 2 cups cooked brown rice, chilled
- 3 tablespoons gochujang
- 1 cup Kimchi, chopped

Instructions:

Pour the peanut oil into a pan over medium heat.

Cook the eggs for 30 seconds.

Flip and cook for another 15 seconds.

Transfer to a chopping board and slice into smaller pieces.

Pour 1 tablespoon vegetable oil to a pan over medium heat.

Cook the garlic, scallions and ginger for 30 seconds.

Stir in the pork and cook while stirring for 2 minutes.

Add the carrots and zucchini.

Cook for 3 minutes.

Transfer to a plate.

Add the remaining oil to the pan.

Fry the rice for 2 minutes.

Put the eggs, veggie and pork back to the pan.

Stir in the sauce and Kimchi.

Mix well.

Serve warm.

Nutrients per Serving:

- Calories 401
- Fat 14.5 g
- Saturated fat 3.3 g
- Carbohydrates 37.6 g
- Fiber 4.8 g
- Protein 29.3 g
- Cholesterol 153 mg
- Sugars 7 g
- Sodium 554 mg
- Potassium 679 mg

Korean Crab Roll Sandwich

If you're looking for a quick, delicious and healthy Korean sandwich recipe, here's one that you should try. What makes this incredibly flavorful is the addition of Korean chili paste called gochujang.

Serving Size: 4

Preparation Cooking Time: 30 minutes

Ingredients:

- ¼ cup rice vinegar
- Salt to taste
- 1 cup cucumber, sliced thinly
- 2 tablespoons shallot, minced
- 2 tablespoons gochujang
- ¼ cup light mayonnaise
- 8 oz. crab meat
- 4 hot dog buns, toasted
- 4 lettuce leaves

Instructions:

Combine the salt and vinegar in a bowl.

Toss the cucumber in this mixture and soak for 20 minutes.

Drain and transfer to another bowl.

Take 1 tablespoon of the vinegar and stir in the shallot, gochujang and mayonnaise.

Add the crabmeat and mix.

Add the lettuce to the buns.

Top with the crab mixture and cucumber.

Nutrients per Serving:

- Calories 293
- Fat 13.3 g
- Saturated fat 2 g
- Carbohydrates 29 g
- Fiber 4 g
- Protein 16.8 g
- Cholesterol 46 mg
- Sugars 7 g
- Sodium 731 mg
- Potassium 193 mg
-

Korean Deviled Eggs

If you love making deviled eggs, for sure, you'll love this Korean version, in which you will combine the egg yolks with Kimchi, yogurt, shallots and mustard.

Serving Size: 24

Preparation Cooking Time: 30 minutes

Ingredients:

- 12 hard-boiled eggs, peeled, cut in half
- 2 tablespoons Kimchi, chopped
- ¼ cup mayonnaise
- ¼ cup Greek yogurt
- 1 tablespoon shallot, minced
- 2 teaspoons gochujang
- 2 teaspoons Dijon mustard
- Salt and pepper to taste
- 1 teaspoon white wine vinegar
- 2 scallion greens, chopped

Instructions:

Scoop the egg yolks from the eggs.

Add to a bowl.

Stir in the rest of the ingredients.

Mix well.

Scoop a tablespoon of the mixture on top of the egg whites.

Refrigerate for 15 minutes and serve.

Nutrients per Serving:

- Calories 48
- Fat 3.2 g
- Saturated fat 0.9 g
- Carbohydrates 1.1 g
- Fiber 1 g
- Protein 3.5 g
- Cholesterol 94 mg
- Sugars 1 g
- Sodium 92 mg
- Potassium 39 mg

Cod Broccolini in Chili Paste

This recipe calls for cooking cod and broccolini in packets. The packet seals not only the flavor but also the moisture, producing excellent results.

Serving Size: 4

Preparation Cooking Time: 45 minutes

Ingredients:

- Cooking spray
- 1 tablespoon vegetable oil
- 2 cloves garlic, crushed and minced
- 4 scallions, chopped
- 1 tablespoon ginger, minced
- 2 cups brown rice, cooked
- 1 bunch broccolini
- 4 cod fillets
- Salt and pepper to taste
- 2 tablespoons light mayonnaise
- 2 tablespoons gochujang

Instructions:

Preheat your oven to 450 degrees F.

Spray foil sheets with oil.

Pour the oil in a pan over medium heat.

Cook the garlic, ginger and scallions for 1 minute.

Add the brown rice and cook for 1 minute.

Place the rice mixture on top of the foil sheet.

Top with the broccolini and fish. Season with salt and pepper.

Mix the mayonnaise and gochujang.

Spread this mixture on top of the cod.

Fold and seal the packets.

Bake in the oven for 15 minutes.

Nutrients per Serving:

- Calories 288
- Fat 6.4 g
- Saturated fat 1.1 g
- Carbohydrates 32.7 g
- Fiber 3 g
- Protein 23.9 g
- Cholesterol 57 mg
- Sugars 3 g
- Sodium 624 mg
- Potassium 574 mg

Steak in Lettuce Cups

This is another version of the popular Korean steak lettuce wraps, but what makes this one different is the addition of Kimchi, yogurt and shredded carrots.

Serving Size: 4

Preparation Cooking Time: 40 minutes

Ingredients:

- 1 lb. flank steak
- Salt and pepper to taste
- 1 cup cucumber, diced
- 6 cherry tomatoes, sliced in half
- ¼ cup shallot, chopped
- 1 tablespoon fresh mint, chopped
- 1 tablespoon fresh basil, chopped
- 1 tablespoon fresh cilantro, chopped
- 1 tablespoon brown sugar
- 2 tablespoons low-sodium soy sauce
- 2 tablespoons freshly squeezed lime juice
- ½ teaspoon red pepper flakes
- Lettuce leaves

Instructions:

Preheat your grill.

Season the steak with the salt and pepper.

Grill the steak for 7 minutes per side.

Place on a cutting board.

Let sit for 5 minutes before slicing.

Mix the steak with the maintaining ingredients except the lettuce.

Top the lettuce leaves with the beef mixture and roll.

Nutrients per Serving:

- Calories 202
- Fat 6.5 g
- Saturated fat 2.4 g
- Carbohydrates 9.4 g
- Fiber 1.4 g
- Protein 26.3 g
- Cholesterol 70 mg
- Sugars 5 g
- Sodium 481 mg
- Potassium 665 mg

Korean Chicken Soup

Chicken soup is the go-to comfort food whenever someone's not feeling well. This Korean version is just as nice and comforting but with a little bit of zing.

Serving Size: 6

Preparation Cooking Time: 35 minutes

Ingredients:

- 8 cups low-sodium chicken broth
- 2 tablespoons ginger, grated
- 2 tablespoons garlic, chopped
- ½ cup white rice
- 1 teaspoon sesame oil, toasted
- 1 teaspoon hot sauce
- 1 tablespoon low-sodium soy sauce
- 1 cup cooked chicken, shredded
- 1 tablespoon sesame seeds, toasted
- 2 stalks scallions, chopped

Instructions:

Pour the broth into a Dutch oven.

Add the ginger and garlic.

Bring to a boil.

Stir in the rice.

Reduce heat and simmer for 15 minutes.

Add the oil, hot sauce and soy sauce.

Stir in the chicken.

Remove from heat and pour into serving bowls.

Sprinkle the sesame seeds and scallions on top before serving.

Nutrients per Serving:

- Calories 149
- Fat 2.5 g
- Saturated fat 0.5 g
- Carbohydrates 17.9 g
- Fiber 0.6 g
- Protein 13.5 g
- Cholesterol 20 mg
- Sugars 1 g
- Sodium 857 mg
- Potassium 392 mg

Sesame Spinach

This recipe is a type of "namul", a group of Korean side dishes of seasoned veggies. In this one, you will season spinach with garlic and sesame seeds.

Serving Size: 4

Preparation Cooking Time: 30 minutes

Ingredients:

- ¼ cup water
- 1 lb. baby spinach
- 2 teaspoons sesame oil
- 2 teaspoons low-sodium soy sauce
- 1 clove garlic, crushed and minced
- 1 tablespoon sesame seeds, toasted

Instructions:

Pour the water into a pan over high heat.

Cook the spinach for 3 minutes.

Drain on a colander.

Squeeze excess water.

Chop the baby spinach.

Stir in the rest of the ingredients.

Nutrients per Serving:

- Calories 56
- Fat 3.6 g
- Saturated fat 0.5 g
- Carbohydrates 4.3 g
- Fiber 2.4 g
- Protein 3.2 g
- Cholesterol 85 mg
- Sugars 1 g
- Sodium 151 mg
- Potassium 425 mg

Beef Broccoli Stir Fry

What makes this beef and broccoli stir fry different from those you've tasted before is that this one comes with mushrooms and is seasoned with gochujang, giving it a distinct Korean taste. Serve with noodles or brown rice.

Serving Size: 4

Preparation Cooking Time: 30 minutes

Ingredients:

Sauce

- 2 tablespoons freshly squeezed lemon juice
- ¼ cup gochujang
- 1 tablespoon dry sherry
- 1 tablespoon soy sauce
- 1 tablespoon fresh ginger, grated
- 2 teaspoons sugar
- 1 tablespoon sesame oil, toasted

Stir-Fry

- 3 tablespoons vegetable oil, divided
- 1 lb. flank steak, fat trimmed and sliced into strips
- 1 tablespoons scallions, sliced
- 4 cups broccoli florets
- 4 cups mushrooms, sliced
- 3 cloves garlic, crushed and minced

Instructions:

Combine the sauce ingredients in a bowl. Mix well.

Pour 1 tablespoon vegetable oil into a pan over medium heat.

Cook the steak for 3 minutes, stirring frequently.

Transfer on a plate.

Add 1 tablespoon oil to the pan.

Add the scallions and broccoli and cook while stirring for 2 minutes.

Add the remaining oil.

Stir fry the mushrooms and garlic for 3 minutes.

Put the steak back to the pan.

Stir in the reserved sauce.

Simmer for 2 minutes.

Nutrients per Serving:

- Calories 341
- Fat 20.4 g
- Saturated fat 4.6 g
- Carbohydrates 12.3 g
- Fiber 3.6 g
- Protein 29 g
- Cholesterol 70 mg
- Sugars 3 g
- Sodium 526 mg
- Potassium 914 mg

Korean Turkey Burger

Yes, Koreans have their own way of making burgers. If you are fond of eating Kimchi, for sure, you are going to enjoy this filling and healthy snack.

Serving Size: 4

Preparation Cooking Time: 30 minutes

Ingredients:

- 1 lb. lean ground turkey

- 1 teaspoon sesame oil, toasted

- 8 teaspoons Korean chili paste, divided

- 3 scallions, chopped

- Cooking spray

- 2 tablespoons light mayonnaise

- 4 whole wheat burger buns

- 1 cup Kimchi

- 12 cucumber slices

Instructions:

Preheat your grill.

In a bowl, mix the turkey, oil, 5 teaspoons chili paste and scallions.

Form patties from the mixture.

Spray the grill rack with oil.

Grill the turkey burgers for 3 minutes per side.

Blend the remaining chili paste and mayo in a bowl.

Spread the spicy mayo on the burger buns.

Add the grilled turkey burger and top with the Kimchi and cucumber.

Top with the other bread slice and serve.

Nutrients per Serving:

- Calories 341
- Fat 11.9 g
- Saturated fat 2.7 g
- Carbohydrates 33.2 g
- Fiber 5.1 g
- Protein 27.6 g
- Cholesterol 67 mg
- Sugars 8 g
- Sodium 782 mg
- Potassium 441 mg

Cucumber Kimchi

When you think of Kimchi, you immediately imagine fermented cabbage. But did you know that you can make another version using cucumbers? Check out this quick and easy recipe.

Serving Size: 6

Preparation Cooking Time: 12 hours and 20 minutes

Ingredients:

- 8 oz. cucumbers, sliced into half rounds
- 1 teaspoon salt
- 2 stalks scallions, chopped
- 1 tablespoon ginger, chopped
- 2 cloves garlic, minced
- 1 tablespoon Korean chili powder
- 2 tablespoons rice vinegar
- ½ teaspoon fish sauce
- 2 teaspoons sugar

Instructions:

Toss the cucumber slices in the salt.

Let stand for 30 minutes.

While waiting, mix the rest of the ingredients in another bowl.

Transfer the cucumbers to a strainer.

Add to the bowl with the vinegar mixture.

Cover the bowl.

Refrigerate for 12 hours.

Nutrients per Serving:

- Calories 8
- Fat 0.1 g
- Saturated fat 0 g
- Carbohydrates 1.9 g
- Fiber 0.3 g
- Protein 0.3 g
- Cholesterol 1 mg
- Sugars 1 g
- Sodium 64 mg
- Potassium 61 mg

Beef Mung Bean Sprouts Stir Fry

Add a little twist to your beef stir fry by throwing in some mung bean sprouts into the mix. Mung bean sprouts add flavor and texture to this stir fry dish.

Serving Size: 2

Preparation Cooking Time: 30 minutes

Ingredients:

- 2 tablespoons low-sodium soy sauce
- 3 tablespoons mirin
- 2 teaspoons cornstarch
- 1 tablespoon vegetable oil
- 8 oz. flank steak, sliced into strips
- 1 teaspoon ginger, chopped
- 2 teaspoons jalapeno pepper, chopped
- 1 tablespoon garlic, chopped
- 4 cups mung bean sprouts
- 6 oz. baby spinach
- ¼ cup fresh cilantro, chopped
- 6 oz. baby spinach
- 1 teaspoon sesame oil, toasted
- ¼ cup fresh cilantro, chopped
- 2 tablespoons sesame seeds, toasted

Instructions:

Pour the soy sauce and mirin into a bowl.

Stir in the cornstarch.

Pour the oil into a pan over medium heat.

Sear the steak for 1 minute per side.

Stir in the ginger, jalapeno and garlic.

Cook while stirring for 30 seconds.

Stir in the spinach and bean sprouts.

Add the mirin mixture.

Cook for 3 minutes.

Add the sesame oil and cilantro.

Garnish with the sesame seeds.

Nutrients per Serving:

- Calories 410
- Fat 17.2 g
- Saturated fat 4 g
- Carbohydrates 28.1 g
- Fiber 6 g
- Protein 34.7 g
- Cholesterol 78 mg
- Sugars 16 g
- Sodium 680 mg
- Potassium 1237 mg

Bulgogi

The term "bulgogi" means fire meat. This popular Korean dish is made of marinated strips of beef usually brisket or rib-eye, grilled or stir-fried.

Serving Size: 6

Preparation Cooking Time: 1 hour and 15 minutes

Ingredients:

- 1 ½ lb. beef sirloin, sliced into strips
- ¼ cup soy sauce
- 2 stalks green onion, chopped
- 3 cloves garlic, minced
- ¼ yellow onion, sliced thinly
- 3 tablespoons white sugar
- ¼ teaspoon ginger, minced
- 2 tablespoons sesame seeds, toasted
- ¼ teaspoon Korean red pepper flakes
- Pepper to taste
- 1 teaspoon honey
- 1 tablespoon sesame oil

Instructions:

Add the steak in a sealable bag.

In a bowl, mix the rest of the ingredients except the honey and oil.

Pour half of the mixture into the bag.

Reserve the other half.

Seal and turn to coat evenly.

Refrigerate for 1 hour.

Pour the oil into a pan over medium heat.

Add the steak into the pan along with the reserved sauce.

Stir in the honey.

Cook for 5 minutes.

Nutrients per Serving:

- Calories 226
- Fat 10.2 g
- Saturated fat 3 g
- Carbohydrates 10.9 g
- Fiber 0.5 g
- Protein 21.4 g
- Cholesterol 49 mg
- Sugars 8 g
- Sodium 844 mg
- Potassium 316 mg

Veggie Bibimbap

Another popular Korean dish, bibimbap is made by mixing rice, meat and veggies. It is usually seasoned with soy sauce, gochujang or doenjang. Most bibimbap are served with fried eggs. Check out this recipe which is ideal for vegetarians.

Serving Size: 3

Preparation Cooking Time: 50 minutes

Ingredients:

- 2 tablespoons sesame oil
- 1 cup zucchini, sliced into strips
- 1 cup carrot, sliced into strips
- 5 oz. mushrooms, sliced
- 6 oz. bamboo shoots, rinsed and drained
- 14 oz. bean sprouts, rinsed and drained
- Salt and pepper to taste
- ¼ cup green onions, sliced
- 2 cups cooked rice
- 2 tablespoons soy sauce
- 1 tablespoon butter
- 3 fried eggs
- 3 teaspoons chili sauce

Instructions:

Pour the oil into a pan over medium heat.

Cook the zucchini and carrots for 5 minutes.

Add the mushrooms, bean sprouts and bamboo shoots.

Cook for another 5 minutes.

Season with the salt.

Transfer the veggies to a bowl.

Add the green onion and rice to the same pan.

Season with the soy sauce and pepper.

Divide the rice into3 bowls.

Top each with vegetables and 1 fried egg.

Serve the rice bowl with the chili sauce.

Nutrients per Serving:

- Calories 395
- Fat 18.8 g
- Saturated fat 5 g
- Carbohydrates 45 g
- Fiber 5.2 g
- Protein 13.6 g
- Cholesterol 196 mg
- Sugars 7 g
- Sodium 1086 mg
- Potassium 500 mg

Korean Cucumber Salad

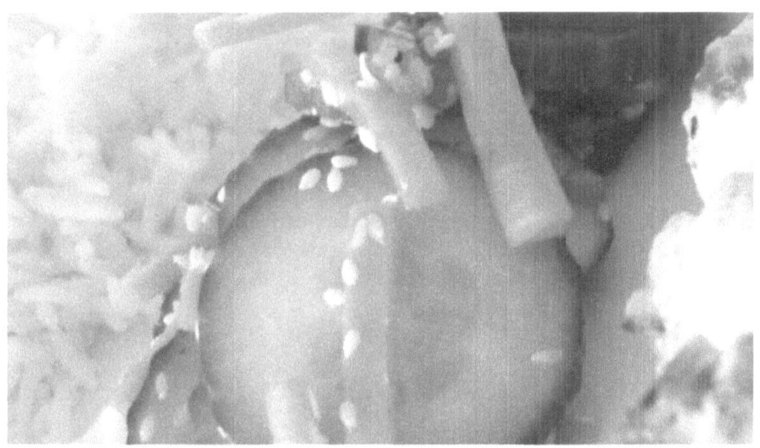

This cucumber salad pairs well with bulgogi, barbecue beef and bibimbap. It's a quick mix of cucumber slices, carrots, sesame seeds and green onions.

Serving Size: 2

Preparation Cooking Time: 25 minutes

Ingredients:

- ¼ cup white vinegar
- ½ teaspoon crushed red pepper
- Pepper to taste
- 1 teaspoon vegetable oil
- 2 tablespoons sesame seeds
- 1 cucumber, sliced into thin rounds
- ½ green onion, chopped
- ½ carrot, sliced into strips

Instructions:

Add the vinegar, red pepper and pepper to a bowl. Mix well.

Pour the oil into a pan over medium heat.

Add the sesame seeds and cook for 5 minutes.

Transfer the sesame seeds into the vinegar.

Stir in the rest of the ingredients.

Cover with foil and refrigerate for 5 minutes before serving.

Nutrients per Serving:

- Calories 98
- Fat 7 g
- Saturated fat 1 g
- Carbohydrates 8.1 g
- Fiber 2.4 g
- Protein 2.6 g
- Cholesterol 0 mg
- Sugars 3 g
- Sodium 14 mg
- Potassium 267 mg

Korean Barbecue Chicken

You'll love the sweet, savory and spicy barbecue sauce used for this grilled chicken recipe. What gives the extra zing is the Korean chili paste. Add more if you can take in more heat.

Serving Size: 12

Preparation Cooking Time: 4 hours and 45 minutes

Ingredients:

- ¼ cup water
- ¼ cup soy sauce
- ¼ cup sugar
- ¼ teaspoon ground ginger
- 2 teaspoons Korean chili paste
- ¼ teaspoon onion powder
- ½ tablespoon lemon juice
- 3 lb. chicken thighs

Instructions:

In a pan over medium heat, add the water, soy sauce, sugar, ginger, and onion powder.

Stir well and bring to a boil.

Reduce heat and simmer for 5 minutes.

Remove from the stove.

Stir in the chili paste and lemon juice.

Transfer the mixture to a bowl.

Add the chicken to the bowl.

Turn to coat evenly.

Cover with foil and refrigerate for 4 hours.

Preheat your grill.

1Grill the chicken for 5 minutes per side.

Nutrients per Serving:

- Protein 0.3 g
- Calories 20
- Cholesterol 0 mg
- Carbohydrates 4.9 g
- Saturated fat 0 g
- Fat 0.1 g
- Fiber 0.1 g
- Sugars 4 g
- Sodium 304 mg
- Potassium 13 mg

Chicken Bulgogi

If you like the sweet and salty flavors of bulgogi but would like to tone down on red meat intake, try this quick and easy chicken bulgogi recipe.

Serving Size: 4

Preparation Cooking Time: 30 minutes

Ingredients:

- 2 tablespoons brown sugar
- 5 tablespoons low-sodium soy sauce
- 1 onion, chopped
- 2 tablespoons garlic, minced
- 1 tablespoon sesame seeds
- 2 tablespoons sesame oil
- Salt and pepper to taste
- ½ teaspoon cayenne
- 1 lb. chicken breast fillets, sliced into strips
- Chopped chives

Instructions:

Combine all the ingredients except the chicken in a bowl.

Pour the mixture into a pan over medium heat.

Stir in the chicken.

Toss to coat evenly with the sauce.

Cook for 15 minutes.

Garnish with the chives before serving.

Nutrients per Serving:

- Calories 269
- Fat 11.6 g
- Saturated fat 2.1 g
- Carbohydrates 13.2 g
- Fiber 0.7 g
- Protein 27.5 g
- Cholesterol 69 mg
- Sugars 9 g
- Sodium 1230 mg
- Potassium 311 mg

Korean Crispy Fried Chicken

This isn't like your ordinary fried chicken. Aside from the crispiness, you'll love that it bursts with so much flavor.

Serving Size: 4

Preparation Cooking Time: 4 hours and 30 minutes

Ingredients:

Marinade

- 1 lb. chicken thighs
- Salt and pepper to taste
- 1 onion, grated
- 4 cloves garlic, crushed and minced

Batter

- ½ cup flour
- 1 cup cornstarch
- Salt and pepper to taste
- 1 teaspoon sugar
- 1 cup cold water
- Oil

Instructions:

Season the chicken with the salt, pepper, onion and garlic.

Cover with cling wrap and refrigerate for 4 hours.

Pour the oil into a pan over medium high heat.

In a bowl, mix the flour, cornstarch, salt, pepper and sugar.

Gradually add the cold water into the flour mixture.

Coat the chicken with the batter.

Fry in hot oil for 4 to 5 minutes or until golden and crispy.

Let cool before serving.

Nutrients per Serving:

- Calories 476
- Fat 23.8 g
- Saturated fat 4.8 g
- Carbohydrates 45.4 g
- Fiber 1.6 g
- Protein 18.6 g
- Cholesterol 71 mg
- Sugars 2 g
- Sodium 1150 mg
- Potassium 227 mg

Spicy Pork

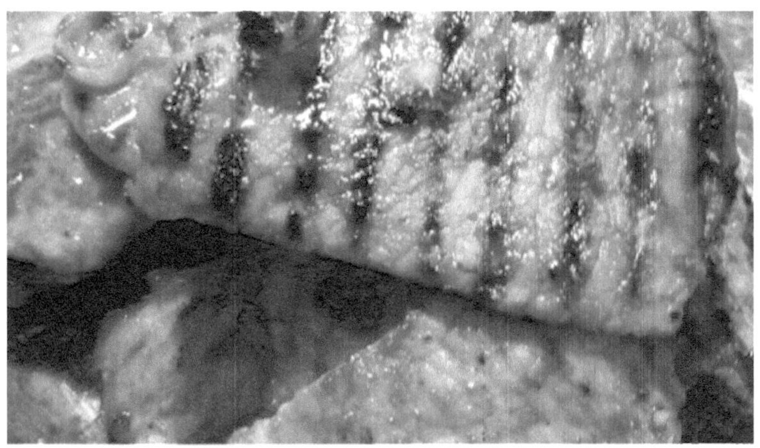

Serve this spicy pork as main course with brown rice, noodles or salad.

Serving Size: 8

Preparation Cooking Time: 4 hours

Ingredients:

- ½ cup gochujang
- 2 tablespoons soy sauce
- ¼ cup rice wine vinegar
- 2 tablespoons red pepper flakes
- 3 tablespoons ginger, minced
- 3 tablespoons garlic, minced
- 3 tablespoons white sugar
- Pepper to taste
- 1 onion, sliced into rings
- 3 stalks green onion, sliced
- 2 lb. pork loin, sliced
- ¼ cup vegetable oil

Instructions:

Add all the ingredients except pork and oil into a large bowl.

Mix well.

Stir in the pork.

Cover with foil.

Marinate in the refrigerator for 3 hours.

Pour the oil into a pan over medium heat.

Cook the pork slices for 3 minutes per side.

Nutrients per Serving:

- Calories 300
- Fat 17.3 g
- Saturated fat 4 g
- Carbohydrates 16.8 g
- Fiber 1 g
- Protein 19.2 g
- Cholesterol 55 mg
- Sugars 8 g
- Sodium 390 mg
- Potassium 377 mg

Miso Soup

This miso soup only takes 35 minutes or less to prepare. But the results are outstanding! You'll definitely enjoy every sip of this warm and comforting soup.

Serving Size: 4

Preparation Cooking Time: 35 minutes

Ingredients:

- 4 cups water
- 1 tablespoon garlic paste
- ½ tablespoon gochujang
- ½ tablespoon dashi granules
- 3 tablespoons Korean bean curd paste
- 1 onion, chopped
- ¼ lb. mushrooms, sliced
- 1 potato, sliced into cubes
- 1 zucchini, sliced into cubes
- 12 oz. soft tofu, sliced

Instructions:

Add the water, garlic paste, gochujang, dashi granules and bean curd paste into a pot over medium high heat.

Mix well.

Bring to a boil.

Stir in the onion and veggies.

Boil for 5 more minutes.

Add the tofu and reduce heat.

Simmer for 20 minutes or until vegetables are tender.

Nutrients per Serving:

- Calories 158
- Fat 4.1 g
- Saturated fat 1 g
- Carbohydrates 21.6 g
- Fiber 3.4 g
- Protein 9.1 g
- Cholesterol 0 mg
- Sugars 5 g
- Sodium 641 mg
- Potassium 545 mg

Jap Chae

Your taste buds will certainly be delighted with these savory noodles that you can serve with grilled ribs, barbecue beef or chicken teriyaki.

Serving Size: 2

Preparation Cooking Time: 40 minutes

Ingredients:

- Water
- ½ lb. Korean dang myun noodles
- 1 teaspoon sesame oil
- 2 teaspoons white sugar
- 2 tablespoons soy sauce
- 1 tablespoon vegetable oil
- ¾ cup onions, sliced thinly
- 2 cloves garlic, crushed and minced
- ½ lb. asparagus, sliced thinly
- 2 carrots, sliced into strips
- ½ cup shiitake mushrooms, sliced
- 3 green onions, chopped
- 1 tablespoon sesame seeds
- 1 ½ teaspoons sesame oil

Instructions:

Fill your pot with water.

Place on high heat and bring to a boil.

Add the noodles and cook for 5 minutes.

Drain and rinse under cool running water.

Toss the noodles in 1 teaspoon sesame oil. Set aside.

In a bowl, mix the sugar and soy sauce. Set aside.

Pour the vegetable oil into a pan over medium heat.

Cook the onion, garlic, asparagus and carrots for 5 minutes.

Stir in the mushrooms and green onions.

Cook for 30 seconds.

Add the soy sauce mixture and noodles.

Cook for 3 minutes.

Remove from the heat.

Stir in the sesame seeds and remaining sesame oil.

Nutrients per Serving:

- Calories 673
- Fat 17.3 g
- Saturated fat 2 g
- Carbohydrates 117.2 g
- Fiber 10.7 g
- Protein 17.3 g
- Cholesterol 0 mg
- Sugars 13 g
- Sodium 1639 mg
- Potassium 1293 mg

Korean Spicy Chicken Wings

It's always a great idea to serve spicy chicken wings when guests come over to your home whether for a casual visitor for a special occasion. Here's a recipe that adds a little bit more to your regular spicy chicken wings.

Serving Size: 6

Preparation Cooking Time: 45 minutes

Ingredients:

- 3 tablespoons barbeque sauce
- 1 cup reduced-sodium soy sauce
- ¼ cup ketchup
- ¾ cup brown sugar
- 2 tablespoons garlic, crushed and minced
- 1 tablespoon chili garlic sauce
- 1 teaspoon ginger, grated
- 1 tablespoon rice wine vinegar
- 1 teaspoon sesame oil
- Pepper to taste
- 1 tablespoon cornstarch
- 1 tablespoon water
- Oil
- 4 lb. chicken wings
- Lemon pepper seasoning to taste

Instructions:

In a large bowl, combine the barbecue sauce, soy sauce, ketchup, sugar, garlic, chili garlic sauce, ginger, vinegar, oil and pepper.

Mix well.

Transfer the mixture to a pan over medium heat.

Bring to a boil.

Mix the cornstarch and water.

Stir into the sauce.

Reduce heat and simmer for 1 minute.

Remove from the stove and set aside.

Pour the oil into a deep fryer.

Sprinkle both sides of the wings with lemon pepper seasoning.

Fry the chicken wings for 7 to 8 minutes or until golden crispy.

Put the chicken wings on a strainer to drain.

Transfer to the bowl with the sauce.

Toss to coat evenly and then serve.

Nutrients per Serving:

- Calories 459
- Fat 22.5 g
- Saturated fat 3.9 g
- Carbohydrates 39.1 g
- Fiber 0.8 g
- Protein 25.5 g
- Cholesterol 64 mg
- Sugars 32 g
- Sodium 1260 mg
- Potassium 350 mg

Slow Cooked Pork

Tender succulent pork chops that are both savory and spicy—something to enjoy on a busy weeknight as this dish can be made ahead of time. Serve with brown rice, noodles or salad.

Serving Size: 6

Preparation Cooking Time: 5 hours and 10 minutes

Ingredients:

- 6 boneless pork chops
- Salt and pepper to taste
- 4 cloves garlic, crushed
- ½ cup reduced-sodium chicken stock
- 1 tablespoon Korean chili bean paste
- ½ cup reduced-sodium soy sauce

Instructions:

Sprinkle both sides of the pork chops with the salt and pepper.

In the slow cooker, add and mix the rest of the ingredients.

Add the pork chops and coat evenly with the sauce.

Seal the pot.

Cook on low for 5 hours.

Nutrients per Serving:

- Calories 142
- Fat 6.7 g
- Saturated fat 2 g
- Carbohydrates 3.5 g
- Fiber 0.2 g
- Protein 16 g
- Cholesterol 39 mg
- Sugars 1 g
- Sodium 747 mg
- Potassium 266 mg

Korean Sushi

In this recipe, you will learn to make Korean sushi otherwise known as "kimbap". For sure, you'll find yourself preparing this recipe more often.

Serving Size: 4

Preparation Cooking Time: 1 hour

Ingredients:

- 1 ½ cups water
- 1 cup sushi rice, rinsed and drained
- Salt to taste
- 1 tablespoon sesame oil
- 2 eggs, beaten
- 4 sheets sushi nori
- 1 carrot, sliced into long thin strips
- 1 cucumber, sliced into long thin strips
- 4 slices ham, sliced into long thin strips
- 4 slices cheese, sliced into long thin strips
- 2 teaspoons sesame oil

Instructions:

Add the water and rice into a small pot.

Bring to a boil and then reduce heat to simmer for 13 to 14 minutes.

Transfer the rice to a baking pan and let cool.

Sprinkle with the salt and drizzle with the sesame oil.

Add the eggs to a pan over medium heat.

Cook without stirring to get a flat and firm layer of egg.

Transfer to a cutting board.

Slice into long strips.

Spread the nori sheets on a flat working surface.

Spread the rice on top but leave a half inch space at the top.

Arrange the egg, carrot, cucumber, ham and cheese on top.

Roll to form a cylinder.

Brush with the remaining oil and slice each roll into six pieces.

Nutrients per Serving:

- Calories 354
- Fat 15.2 g
- Saturated fat 6 g
- Carbohydrates 41.2 g
- Fiber 1.4 g
- Protein 11.9 g
- Cholesterol 113 mg
- Sugars 2 g
- Sodium 510 mg
- Potassium 96 mg

Korean Baby Potatoes

Korean baby potatoes are a wonderful option for side dish that you can prepare in as quickly as 25 minutes.

Serving Size: 4

Preparation Cooking Time: 25 minutes

Ingredients:

- 2 tablespoons vegetable oil
- 1 ½ lb. baby potatoes, sliced into quarters
- 2 tablespoons ketchup
- 2 ½ tablespoons reduced-sodium soy sauce
- 2 tablespoons corn syrup
- ½ cup water
- 1 tablespoon garlic, crushed and minced
- 1/8 teaspoon red pepper flakes
- 1 ½ tablespoons white sugar
- 1 teaspoon sesame seeds

Instructions:

Pour the oil into a pan over medium heat.

Cook the potatoes for 6 to 8 minutes.

In a bowl, mix the rest of the ingredients except the sesame seeds.

Drain the oil from the pan.

Pour the sauce over the cooked baby potatoes.

Coat evenly.

Reduce heat and simmer for 8 minutes.

Garnish with the sesame seeds before serving.

Nutrients per Serving:

- Calories 259
- Fat 7.4 g
- Saturated fat 1 g
- Carbohydrates 46 g
- Fiber 4 g
- Protein 4.4 g
- Cholesterol 0 mg
- Sugars 11 g
- Sodium 433 mg
- Potassium 778 mg

Korean Tofu Veggie Soup

Koreans love soup. One of the most popular Korean soups that you definitely have to try is this one that's made with tofu, radish, squash and fermented soybean paste. It's spicy, filling, delicious and comforting.

Serving Size: 4

Preparation Cooking Time: 35 minutes

Ingredients:

- 3 cups low-sodium beef broth
- ¼ cup fermented soybean paste (doenjang)
- 5 cloves garlic, crushed and minced
- 4 pieces dried kelp (dashi kombu)
- 1 lb. squash, sliced
- 1 lb. Napa cabbage, chopped coarsely
- 1 lb. radish, sliced
- 16 oz. tofu, sliced into cubes
- 1 chili pepper, sliced
- 2 stalks green onions, sliced

Instructions:

Pour the beef broth into a soup pot over medium heat.

Add the fermented soybean paste and mix until dissolved.

Stir in the garlic and kelp.

Bring to a boil.

Add the squash, cabbage, radish and tofu.

Continue boiling for 2 minutes.

Reduce heat and simmer for 5 minutes.

Add the chili pepper and green onions.

Simmer for 2 minutes.

Discard the kelp before serving in soup bowls.

Nutrients per Serving:

- Calories 289
- Fat 12.3 g
- Saturated fat 1.8 g
- Carbohydrates 24.7 g
- Fiber 9.1 g
- Protein 26.4 g
- Cholesterol 0 mg
- Sugars 8 g
- Sodium 661 mg
- Potassium 1304 mg

Korean Crab Cake

Crab cakes infused with Korean flavors—something you and your family will look forward to. Serve these with chili garlic sauce and steamed veggies.

Serving Size: 4

Preparation Cooking Time: 50 minutes

Ingredients:

- 6 oz. crabmeat
- ¼ cup light mayonnaise
- 1 tablespoon fresh ginger, chopped
- 2 tablespoons fresh cilantro, chopped
- 3 oz. shrimp, chopped
- 1 ½ cups breadcrumbs, divided
- 2 teaspoons fish sauce
- Salt and pepper to taste
- 1 ½ tablespoons peanut oil

Instructions:

In a large bowl, mix the crabmeat, mayo, ginger, cilantro, shrimp, ½ cup breadcrumbs and fish sauce.

Sprinkle with the salt and pepper.

Form patties from the mixture.

Pour the peanut oil into a pan over medium heat.

Cook the crab cakes for 4 to 5 minutes per side or until golden and crispy.

Nutrients per Serving:

- Calories 254
- Fat 17.4 g
- Saturated fat 3 g
- Carbohydrates 9.6 g
- Fiber 0.5 g
- Protein 14.5 g
- Cholesterol 75 mg
- Sugars 1 g
- Sodium 620 mg
- Potassium 235 mg

Shrimp Porridge

Porridges are a staple among many Asian cuisines. In Korea, one of the most loved porridges is this recipe made with shrimp and white rice. It's very simple yet flavorful and filling.

Serving Size: 3

Preparation Cooking Time: 2 hours and 15 minutes

Ingredients:

- 2 cups white rice
- 1 tablespoon sesame oil
- 1 tablespoon rice wine
- 9 oz. shrimp, peeled and deveined
- 12 cups water
- Salt to taste

Instructions:

Rinse the rice and soak in water for 2 hours.

Pour the oil into a pan over medium heat.

Cook the shrimp for 1 minute.

Add the rice wine.

Stir in the rice.

Pour the water and then bring to a boil.

Reduce heat and simmer for 10 minutes, stirring frequently.

Season with the salt before serving.

Nutrients per Serving:

- Calories 586
- Fat 6.8 g
- Saturated fat 1 g
- Carbohydrates 99.6 g
- Fiber 1.6 g
- Protein 25.9 g
- Cholesterol 128 mg
- Sugars 0 g
- Sodium 159 mg
- Potassium 308 mg

Spicy Potatoes with Red Bell Pepper

Spicy potatoes with chopped red bell pepper, sesame seeds and green onions are a traditional side dish in Korea. To prepare this dish, you only need 25 minutes.

Serving Size: 4

Preparation Cooking Time: 25 minutes

Ingredients:

- Cayenne pepper to taste
- 1 ½ tablespoons reduced-sodium soy sauce
- 1 ½ tablespoons vegetable oil
- 3 potatoes, sliced into cubes
- 1 red bell pepper, chopped
- 2 teaspoons sesame seeds
- 4 stalks green onions, chopped

Instructions:

Dissolve the cayenne pepper in the soy sauce. Set aside.

Pour the oil into a pan over medium heat.

Add the potatoes and cook for 5 minutes.

Stir in the red bell pepper, sesame seeds and green onions.

Cook for 1 minute.

Add the reserved sauce into the pan and cook until the sauce has been reduced or absorbed by the potatoes.

Nutrients per Serving:

- Calories 198
- Fat 6.2 g
- Saturated fat 1 g
- Carbohydrates 32.3 g
- Fiber 5 g
- Protein 4.6 g
- Cholesterol 0 mg
- Sugars 3 g
- Sodium 352 mg
- Potassium 822 mg

Korean Kebab

Get a taste of the Korean version of kebab, which produces succulent and tender meat that's bursting with spices and flavors.

Serving Size: 6

Preparation Cooking Time: 3 hours and 40 minutes

Ingredients:

- ¼ cup low-sodium soy sauce
- 1 tablespoon peanut butter
- ¼ cup vegetable oil
- 1 clove garlic, crushed
- 2 tablespoons green onion, chopped
- Salt and pepper to taste
- Red chili powder to taste
- 1 teaspoon sesame seeds
- 1 ½ lb. pork tenderloin, sliced into cubes
- 1 onion, sliced
- 8 oz. mushrooms
- 1 red bell pepper, sliced
- 1 zucchini, sliced

Instructions:

In a bowl, mix the soy sauce, peanut butter, oil, garlic, green onion, salt, pepper, chili powder and sesame seeds.

Take 3 tablespoons of the sauce and set aside.

Add the pork cubes into the marinade.

Turn to coat evenly.

Cover the bowl with foil.

Marinate in the refrigerator for 3 hours.

Preheat your oven to 400 degrees F.

Line your baking pan with foil.

Thread the pork cubes into skewers alternating with the veggies.

Add to the baking sheet.

Pour the reserved sauce over the kebabs.

Bake in the oven for 30 minutes.

Nutrients per Serving:

- Calories 237
- Fat 13.4 g
- Saturated fat 3 g
- Carbohydrates 8.9 g
- Fiber 2.2 g
- Protein 21.2 g
- Cholesterol 49 mg
- Sugars 4 g
- Sodium 685 mg
- Potassium 618 mg

Kimchi Pancake

Both the taste and texture will tantalize your taste buds to no end. Serve these fried eggs, spicy sauce or grilled chicken or beef.

Serving Size: 4

Preparation Cooking Time: 35 minutes

Ingredients:

- 12 oz. Kimchi
- ½ teaspoon sesame oil
- ¼ cup water
- 1 egg
- Salt to taste
- 1 teaspoon brown sugar
- ½ cup green onions, sliced thinly
- ¾ cup all-purpose flour
- 1 tablespoon vegetable oil

Instructions:

Add the Kimchi to a strainer to drain but reserve the Kimchi juice.

Chop the Kimchi and set aside.

In a bowl, mix 3 tablespoons of the Kimchi juice with the sesame oil, water, egg, salt and brown sugar.

Mix well.

Stir in the Kimchi, green onion, and flour.

Pour the oil into a pan over medium heat.

Cook the batter for 3 minutes per side or until golden and crispy.

Nutrients per Serving:

- Calories 167
- Fat 5.7 g
- Saturated fat 1 g
- Carbohydrates 23.5 g
- Fiber 2 g
- Protein 6.2 g
- Cholesterol 46 mg
- Sugars 3 g
- Sodium 871 mg
- Potassium 290 mg

Korean Chicken Potatoes

Chicken drumsticks, onions, carrots and potatoes cooked in savory spicy sauce made with Korean chili pepper paste, this dish gives you pleasure and zing with every bite.

Serving Size: 4

Preparation Cooking Time: 1 hour

Ingredients:

- 2 ½ pounds chicken drumsticks
- 2 potatoes, sliced into cubes
- 2 carrots, sliced into cubes
- 1 onion, sliced
- 5 cloves garlic, crushed
- ¼ cup water
- ½ cup soy sauce
- 2 tablespoons white sugar
- 3 tablespoons gochujang

Instructions:

In a pot over medium heat, combine all the ingredients.

Mix well.

Bring to a boil.

Reduce heat and simmer for 45 minutes.

Serve with rice.

Nutrients per Serving:

- Calories 447
- Fat 14.1 g
- Saturated fat 3 g
- Carbohydrates 54.7 g
- Fiber 2 g
- Protein 25.6 g
- Cholesterol 59 mg
- Sugars 3 g
- Sodium 445 mg
- Potassium 750 mg

Korean Fried Rice

Korean fried rice, which they call "omni rice", is so good you don't have to pair it with anything to enjoy it. But you can serve it with vegetables or grilled meat if you like.

Serving Size: 4

Preparation Cooking Time: 1 hour and 20 minutes

Ingredients:

- 2 tablespoons vegetable oil, divided
- 2 cups lean ground beef
- 1 onion, chopped
- 1 carrot, sliced into small cubes
- 1 potato, sliced into small cubes
- 1 zucchini, chopped
- Salt and pepper to taste
- 6 cups cooked white rice
- 1 tablespoon sesame seeds
- 4 eggs, beaten
- ¼ cup ketchup

Instructions:

Pour the oil into a pan over medium high heat.

Cook the ground beef for 10 minutes, stirring occasionally.

Drain the beef and transfer to a bowl.

Cook the onion, carrot and potato in the same pan for 6 to 8 minutes.

Add the zucchini and season with the salt.

Cook for 5 minutes.

Stir in the beef and mix well.

Season with the pepper.

Add the cooked rice and cook while stirring for 5 minutes.

Sprinkle with the sesame seeds and cook for another 5 minutes.

Transfer to a serving plate.

In another pan, fry the eggs until firm.

Put the fried eggs on top of the rice.

Drizzle the ketchup on top.

Nutrients per Serving:

- Calories 916
- Fat 22.5 g
- Saturated fat 6 g
- Carbohydrates 143 g
- Fiber 6.2 g
- Protein 32.6 g
- Cholesterol 227 mg
- Sugars 8 g
- Sodium 351 mg
- Potassium 1114 mg

Samgyeopsal

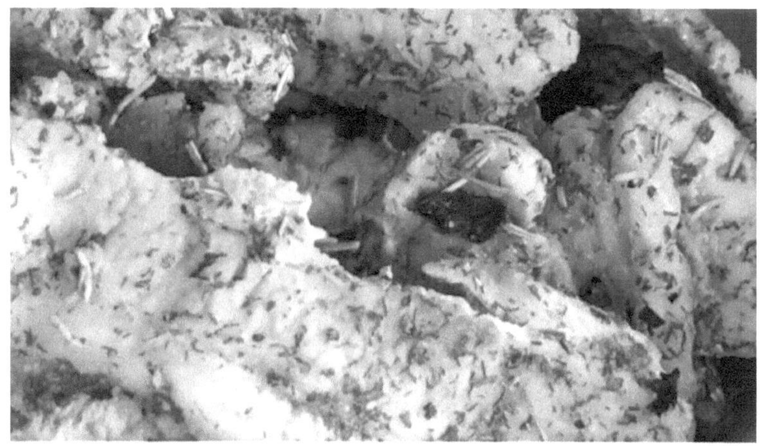

Samgyeopsal is a popular Korean dish made with grilled pork belly. In this recipe, you'll be making one with different herbs and spices.

Serving Size: 6

Preparation Cooking Time: 1 hour

Ingredients:

- 1 teaspoon garlic powder
- 1 teaspoon dried rosemary
- 1 teaspoon dried dill weed
- 1 teaspoon dried thyme
- 2 lb. pork belly strips
- 3 scallions, minced
- 8 cloves garlic, peeled
- 1 cup Kimchi, chopped
- Ssamjang sauce for serving

Instructions:

Combine the garlic powder, rosemary, dill weed and thyme in a bowl.

Sprinkle both sides of the pork belly with this mixture.

Marinate for 15 minutes.

Put a pan over medium heat.

Cook the pork belly until golden brown and crispy.

Drain on a plate lined with paper towel.

Transfer to a cutting board and slice.

In the same pan, cook the scallions, garlic and Kimchi.

Serve the pork belly with the Kimchi mixture and ssamjang sauce.

Nutrients per Serving:

- Calories 349
- Fat 24.1 g
- Saturated fat 7 g
- Carbohydrates 11.5 g
- Fiber 1.7 g
- Protein 20.9 g
- Cholesterol 55 mg
- Sugars 2 g
- Sodium 1594 mg
- Potassium 425 mg

Korean Wontons

Serve these delicious Korean wontons when you're having guests over or when you want something different for dinner time.

Serving Size: 6

Preparation Cooking Time: 1 hour

Ingredients:

- 1 ½ teaspoons vegetable oil
- ½ cup carrots, shredded
- 1 cup bean sprouts
- 2 cups cabbage, chopped
- ¼ lb. ground beef
- ¼ cup green onions, sliced
- 3 cloves garlic, crushed and minced
- 1 egg, beaten
- 1 ½ teaspoons toasted sesame seeds
- 1 ½ teaspoons sesame oil
- ½ teaspoon ground ginger
- Salt and pepper to taste
- 16 oz. wonton wrappers
- Vegetable oil

Instructions:

Pour the oil into a pan over medium high heat.

Cook the carrots, bean sprouts and cabbage for 7 minutes.

Transfer to a bowl.

Add the beef to the same pan.

Cook for 6 minutes.

Drain and stir into the bowl with the veggies.

Stir in the green onion, garlic, egg, sesame seeds, sesame oil, ginger, salt and pepper.

Mix well.

Spoon a tablespoon of this mixture on top of the wonton wrapper.

Moisten the edges with water, fold and seal.

Pour the oil into a pan over medium heat.

Fry the wontons for 1 minute per side or until golden.

Nutrients per Serving:

- Calories 331
- Fat 9 g
- Saturated fat 2 g
- Carbohydrates 47.8 g
- Fiber 2.9 g
- Protein 13.7 g
- Cholesterol 53 mg
- Sugars 1 g
- Sodium 668 mg
- Potassium 220 mg

Korean Pork Celery

This recipe is proof that pork and celery are great together. Cook time is more than an hour, but you only need a few minutes of active preparation.

Serving Size: 4

Preparation Cooking Time: 1 hour and 40 minutes

Ingredients:

- 2 green onions, chopped
- 3 cloves garlic, crushed
- 2 tablespoons fresh ginger, grated
- 2 tablespoons tomato paste
- 4 tablespoons low-sodium soy sauce, divided
- 2 tablespoons white sugar, divided
- 2 tablespoons rice wine
- ¾ teaspoon red pepper flakes, crushed
- 1 tablespoon sesame oil
- 1 lb. pork loin, sliced into strips
- ¼ cup vegetable oil, divided
- 4 stalks celery, sliced into strips (reserve leaves)

Instructions:

Combine the green onion, garlic, ginger, tomato paste, 2 tablespoons soy sauce, sugar, rice wine, ¼ teaspoon red pepper flakes, and sesame oil in a bowl.

Cover with foil.

Marinate in the refrigerator for 1 hour.

Pour 1 tablespoon oil in a pan over medium heat.

Cook the pork for 10 minutes, turning once or twice.

Transfer to a plate.

Pour 1 teaspoon oil in the pan.

Cook the celery and remaining red pepper flakes for 1 minute.

Stir in the remaining soy sauce. Cook for 1 minute.

Add the celery leaves and cook for 3 minutes.

Serve the pork with the celery.

Nutrients per Serving:

- Calories 359
- Fat 24.1 g
- Saturated fat 4 g
- Carbohydrates 12.7 g
- Fiber 1.5 g
- Protein 21.2 g
- Cholesterol 54 mg
- Sugars 8 g
- Sodium 1039 mg
- Potassium 560 mg

Conclusion

Now that you have this book, you can enjoy Korean dishes whenever you want.

Any time you're craving for Korean sushi (kimbap), Korean kebab, bulgogi, beef and vegetable stir-fry, Kimchi, or tofu stew, you simply have to turn to this book and get working in the kitchen.

Even if you're usually busy, you don't have to worry as most of the recipes from this book only require a few minutes of active preparation.

As for the ingredients, you will find most of what you need in Asian food stores and supermarkets.

There is no need for a lot of money to be spent in Asian restaurants when you can prepare the dishes you love in your own kitchen.

About the Author

A native of Albuquerque, New Mexico, Sophia Freeman found her calling in the culinary arts when she enrolled at the Sante Fe School of Cooking. Freeman decided to take a year after graduation and travel around Europe, sampling the cuisine from small bistros and family owned restaurants from Italy to Portugal. Her bubbly personality and inquisitive nature made her popular with the locals in the villages and when she finished her trip and came home, she had made friends for life in the places she had visited. She also came home with a deeper understanding of European cuisine.

Freeman went to work at one of Albuquerque's 5-star restaurants as a sous-chef and soon worked her way up to head chef. The restaurant began to feature Freeman's original dishes as specials on the menu and soon after, she began to write e-books with her recipes. Sophia's dishes mix local flavours with European inspiration making them irresistible to the diners in her restaurant and the online community.

Freeman's experience in Europe didn't just teach her new ways of cooking, but also unique methods of presentation. Using rich sauces, crisp vegetables and meat cooked to perfection, she creates a stunning display as well as a delectable dish. She has won many local awards for her cuisine and she continues to delight her diners with her culinary masterpieces.

Author's Afterthoughts

I want to convey my big thanks to all of my readers who have taken the time to read my book. Readers like you make my work so rewarding and I cherish each and every one of you.

Grateful cannot describe how I feel when I know that someone has chosen my work over all of the choices available online. I hope you enjoyed the book as much as I enjoyed writing it.

Feedback from my readers is how I grow and learn as a chef and an author. Please take the time to let me know your thoughts by leaving a review on Amazon so I and your fellow readers can learn from your experience.

My deepest thanks,

Sophia Freeman

https://sophia.subscribemenow.com/

* * * * ★ ★ ★ ★ * * * *